Break Free

Be True. Be You.

Patrick "Pac Man" Perez

Dr. Raphael Travis Jr., LCSW

Hey Emma!

Break Free

Break Free

Break Free

Patrick "Pac Man" Perez

Patrick "Pac Man" Perez's mission is to empower students to create better futures by making better choices. Patrick's dance is the hook that draws teens into his world so he can help better their world. This native Texan has danced to over 300,000 people across the world, earned his B.A. in Communication Studies and is the author of Mad Skills for Student Success and Bully Breakthrough.

Break Free

The "Doc"

Dr. Raphael Travis explores positive youth development over the life course, adolescent resilience, and youth participation in individual and community change. He blends social work and public health ideas to create meaningful advances in health and well-being.

Break Free

Break Free

> "LIFE IS AN ADVENTURE, AN UNFOLDING
> DISCOVERY OF WHO WE ARE."
>
> -Patrick Perez

Hey There,

As we came to the completion of this book my brain was at a blank about the title. The original title just didn't seem to fit the overall direction of the book. Ha, kinda like life, huh? Maybe your "title" doesn't really fit the story you are living out so far.

Well, as I sat at a Starbucks brainstorming titles with my brother I felt I was just at a dead end. The original title "From Me to We" was great, but not really fitting. I sat in traffic listening to XM's "Chill" channel and still nothing was coming to mind. I wanted a title that would be self explanatory, yet, make sense with the rest of the book.

I wanted a title that would represent the readers who are holding this book. Readers, like you, from all walks of life. I wanted something awesome.

Break Free

I began to think of the awesome people I have met in my life's journey. Not just people who were doing awesome things, but who were just, well...awesome. One buddy popped into mind, a crazy dancer and stunt man who I met while he was still in high school. His name is Josh Vinyard aka "Elusive."

Never mind the fact that he rocked the stage on America's Got Talent or that he was a stuntman in the revised Spiderman 2 movie. Never mind the fact that Josh is one of the sickest dancers I've met (check out www. JoshVinyard.com). The reason I think people like Josh are awesome is simple...he is true to who he is. Any great dancer can get on the floor and show off, but Josh is so authentic to who he is that he can get out there and be a clown on the floor! He is not afraid to be goofy, silly or just downright weird at times.

In my eyes that is awesome. *Awesome is the color of authenticity*. Awesome is so overused in our culture, but it is the only word that I could use to describe my central hope and goal for this book...that you would accept, embrace and be true to who you are in a way that you are excited about who you are. We don't need more people who can just do awesome things, *we need more people who can simply be true to who they are and inspire those around them to do the same.*

If I can talk about one thing that has mattered most to me in my life, it has been the struggle to grow into and accept who I am. Yes, my friends may think I am a freak (no argument there.) However, they still love me. Wherever you are on your journey, I hope by the end of this book you will be just a tad more comfortable in your own skin. The "Doc" and I joined forces on this book for the simple mission of helping "you better understand yourself. I hope that you can smile at the end of each day knowing you have been true to who you are. I hope you can share in this simple statement that I am so blessed to be able to say each day, "I am a freak. I love my life and I am awesoME."

WELL! That title lasted about a week. As I was talking to one of my friends she asked me about the book's progress. I told her the title I came up with and she then asked, "What's it about?" I replied, "Well, in short it is about helping people break free from how others view them and be true to who they are. Bam! BREAK FREE, boyyyyy!! So, there, that is the epic tale behind the title of this book. Roll tide.

Break Free

Awesome Contents

Break Free

> "YOU CAN BE ANYTHING IN THE WORLD,
> IN GOD WE TRUST.
> AN ARCHITECT, DOCTOR, MAYBE AN ACTRESS, BUT
> NOTHING COMES EASY IT TAKES MUCH PRACTICE."
>
> Nas |"I Can"

Each chapter (with the exception of "I Know You, You Know Me") is written by Patrick with insights and end of chapter exercises from "Doc." That way you don't get us mixed up since we do look alike :)

Break Free

Let the Journey Begin

> "IDENTITY IS A PRISON YOU CAN NEVER ESCAPE, BUT THE WAY TO REDEEM YOUR PAST IS NOT TO RUN FROM IT, BUT TO TRY TO UNDERSTAND IT, AND USE IT AS A FOUNDATION TO GROW."
>
> Jay-Z| Decoded

This would prove to be the best $5 I had ever spent! It was 3 pm on Halloween day. Who was I going to be? My original idea was to dress as famed silent film star Charlie Chaplain. For you youngstas who don't know who he was Google him, he was awesome.

I went from Halloween store to Halloween store. When that failed to produce a good costume I began looking in Goodwill stores across town. I couldn't find the famous bowl shaped hat that Charlie Chaplain always wore. Although, I did manage to find the short mustache he had. I figured I could always go as Hitler if all else failed (psssh! yeah, right!)

I gave up on being Charlie Chaplain when I had the epic idea of getting a Barack Obama mask, a cape and some fangs-I could go as Barackula! I found a Barack mask and...

Break Free

whoa! $20?! Are you serious? Yeah, I'm cheap. Goodbye, Barackula. My hunt for who I would become was still on.

After several hours I was drained, my eyes hurt, I was drained and my eyes hurt. I was ready to give up when I decided to try one more Goodwill store. I rummaged through the cluttered aisles. I braved the shelves of discarded pieces that made for a colorful collage of chaos. At that moment my life felt like a colorful collage of chaos!

There were piles of orphaned beards, glasses, leprechaun hats, clown noses, a ripped Darth Vader outfit, vampire fangs... ugh! What will I dress up as?? Who shall I be??

I headed for the exit when I saw one last end cap. The area looked like Wal-Mart had thrown up all over it. I sighed and forced myself to dig into the heap of hopeless artifacts with no expectations of finding my treasure. By this time I didn't know who I wanted to be for Halloween, I had no desire to go to another store, my brain was fried and my soul was fed up.

Fairy wings? No. Cowboy pistols? No. Werewolf mask? No. Reindeer antlers? No. Wait! Reindeer antlers! Waiiittttt for it,think,think,think!

YES! Reindeer antlers! In exactly .0638 seconds I knew who I would be for Halloween!!! Yes!!

I grabbed the reindeer antlers, ran to another aisle where I had seen a clown make up kit with a red nose and headed for the cashier. I paid the incredible amount of $4 for my antlers and clown make up kit and rushed home in a delirious euphoria!

Break Free

I grabbed a Salem High School Viking football t-shirt, safety pinned some poker cards and Uno cards to it. I then duct taped (yeah, duct tape!) some Scrabble pieces and Jinga game pieces to my antlers. I finally put on a cape that I had (yeah, people in Austin sport capes) and taped some paper to it with Hangman and a Crossword puzzle.

While some people may think I was on crack, crazy or just plain weird, *I knew who I wanted to be.* After several hours of shopping, exploring, thinking, whining and ultimately creating my costume I was satisfied. I was *Reindeer Games.* Yes, like the Christmas song says, "They wouldn't let poor Rudolph play any reindeer games."

It took time, but my costume mirrored my two desires: to entertain and impress (even though the impress part was to be questioned.) *I had to dig through a lot of junk in order to become who I wanted to be.* At the end of the day, I was **empowered** and entertaining. Halloween is over, and that costume is buried somewhere, but the experience was well worth it.

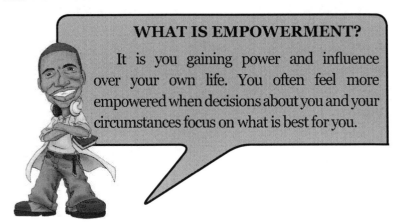

WHAT IS EMPOWERMENT?

It is you gaining power and influence over your own life. You often feel more empowered when decisions about you and your circumstances focus on what is best for you.

Break Free

The question I now have for you is simple- **How much junk are you willing to dig through in order to become the person you want to be?**

Who are you? Scary question, huh? The question of **"Who am I"?** is a question that must be asked time and time again. We let people guess who we are, maybe even label us, but how we see ourselves as is how we will live our lives out.

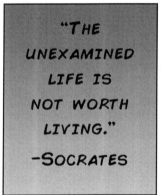
"THE UNEXAMINED LIFE IS NOT WORTH LIVING."
-SOCRATES

Super brain dude and philosopher Socrates once said, "The unexamined life is not worth living." While quite extreme he makes a valid point-we must *examine* who we are.

We cannot just wear a mask that someone else hands us. Our identity is rooted in our experiences, fears, culture, hopes and dreams. **Self-esteem** is what we think of ourselves. *Is your view of yourself a positive one? Does it make you smile or frown? How satisfying is your view of yourself?*

As I walk, stumble, run, dance, hop, crawl and stroll through this journey called life I have seen friends change. I have seen myself change. I grew from a bullied-band nerd in middle and high school into a successful dancer, professional youth speaker and entrepreneur. I saw friends in high school change from loving, caring amigos to cold, violent gang members. People change. *Life is change.*

Break Free

Esteem is how much YOU like YOU! Don't trip about what other people say, only you know you!

As I write this I am enjoying life as a 33-year-old adventurous bachelor. The question of "Who am I?" is still part of my life. Life is a process; becoming who we are is an unfolding discovery. Let's do this, yo!

Time Tells All

1. Grab a watch or use your phone.

2. Give yourself 30 seconds to do the following!

3. Write as many words that you can that describe who you are in the box below.

4. In other words finish the sentence "I am _____" with as many words as you can.

Break Free

5. Write any word, "good" or "bad" - just continue to write whatever comes to mind to complete the sentence for 30 seconds.

6. Ready? Set... Go!!!

I am...

Nicely done! Now, give yourself another 30 seconds and this time write down descriptive, **positive words that you want to be described as**. For example, this could include: **healthy, outgoing, successful, truthful, honest, daring,** etc. **Ready? 30 seconds. GO!**

Break Free

I want to be known as...

All right, last part!

Circle the top 3-5 words that you really want to use
to describe the best version of you – that is, how you are
when at your very best.

Now write only those words below

and tell us who you are!

Break Free

I AM...

"I see you, but how do you see yourself!?"

Break Free

Although not necessarily the TRUE YOU, you can sometimes allow how others label you to influence your self-esteem."

The desires for a strong sense of self, respect in the eyes of others and to have power and recognizable talents are a GOOD thing. **However, you must pay close attention** to HOW you accomplish those goals.

Break Free

Beyond the Battle

> *"EVERY BATTLE BEGINS WITHIN."*
>
> **-Patrick Perez**

Energy, sweat and phat beats filled the room. I couldn't believe that destiny had brought two of the best dancers in the world onto the same stage. Each move...precise. Every beat...annihilated. Sixteen of the best b-boys (e.g. break dancers) from around the world had battled it out in a frenzy of fierce moves and smooth style to make it onto this stage.

Now, in the final round of Red Bull's 2009 BC1 Championship, there were only two rhythmic warriors left standing. Representing the USA was a cat by the name of Daniel "Cloud" Campos from Skill Methodz crew. His outwardly proud Muslim opponent, Lilou, was reppin' the Pockemon Crew from France. Move for move and style for style I think this was one of the dopest battles I have ever seen!

I won't tell you who won, (YouTube "Cloud Vs. Lilou"), but the only thing that caught my attention more than the moves was Cloud's shirt. On the back of his gray sweater were the words: **"The only person you battle in life is yourself."** Dang! If that doesn't make you pause and

Break Free

think please go drink a triple shot of espresso and come back!

The image you carry around of yourself internally will showcase itself in the way you live externally. You will face many battles in life: relational, academic, physical and dramatic-OMG!-say-it-to-my-face-kick-a-squirrel-throw-a-banana type arguments with friends, siblings or parents!

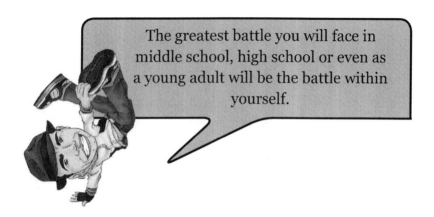

The greatest battle you will face in middle school, high school or even as a young adult will be the battle within yourself.

The question of "Who Am I?" will influence what you do and where you go in life. So, are you ready to dominate this battle? Let's do it. Word to your mom! Oh, and if you want to check out another sick battle YouTube "Cloud vs. Kaku!" Sick I say, sick!

If every battle truly begins within, then you must toughen up your mental muscles. In his book *See You at the Top,* master salesman and legendary speaker Zig Ziglar encourages us to keep a record of our achievements. I want you to think of the 10 best victories you've had in

Break Free

the last few years. These are the highlights of who you are. Examples: passing that evil math test that was so hard, auditioning for a school musical, scoring that date, running your first mile, finishing a long book, finding friends that accept who you are, walking away from a fight, etc. These are your victories and highlights, if it was an achievement to you that is all that matters. Now, write those 10 highlights down in the space below.

1. _____

2. _____

3. _____

4. _____

5. _____

6. _____

7. _____

8. _____

9. _____

10. _____

Break Free

Now, let's flex those mental muscles!

Select your top three victories & write them below:

"Flex those muscles, you're a beast!"

Break Free

I encourage you to keep these top 3 victories somewhere you can see them. Zig Ziglar actually recommended taking all 10 victories, writing them down on a 3 x 5 card and keeping this card on hand so you can pull it out whenever you need some motivation. You can even take a pic and save it to your phone. When you are feeling down or like you need a boost, read over your past victories and be reminded that you are capable of some pretty awesome things! I carry my little 3 x 5 card in my wallet.

Wanna wanna know what's on my card?? Shoot me a message and I'll send you a pic. @patrickpacman on Twitter or patrick@patrickperez.org

Break Free

SEEING BETTER:

- Take pictures of the things that make you feel better when you are feeling "down."

- Take pictures of things or activities that bring you "joy."

- Take pictures of something that seems to bring great "joy" to a person in your life that you care a lot about.

*Edit pictures & make a collage **with www.picmonkey.com***

If you capture video, **create a movie with www. magisto.com or the Magisto app** *(download on your phone) – use songs inspired from today! You can use any photo or video editing software for this activity.*

Break Free

Break Free

The Avatar Experience

Okay, time for a tree-loving hippie moment:

What are the 3 top things you LOVE about yourself? Physical, mental, social, etc. Don't think, just write, now!

1. _

2. _

3. _

Next, what are 3 things about yourself you wish you could change? Write, sucka!

1. _

2. _

3. _

Break Free

With all the social media and on-line living we do it is soooo easy to make ourselves appear perfect.

You can upload a picture that appears flawless, you can tell the world how great you are and how much money you make. I've seen people upload pictures that are so Photoshopped they almost look fake! Ha!

The person behind the avatar, screen name, or profile is the person you really are: the good, the bad and the ugly. We are able to change our whole "appearance" by the clothes we wear, accessories we adorn or even by the car we drive. As much as we wish to show the world how perfect we are, we will all have our faults.

"Technology has caused children to shift away from expressing their self-identities and toward constructing a façade based on the answer to the question, "How can I ensure that others view me positively?"

– Dr. Jim Taylor

In: Parenting/Popular Culture: Media's Externalization of Your Children's Self-identity (www.drjimtaylor.com)

Break Free

People may perceive you a certain way, but only you can show them the true person – **Only you know you!** A few years ago I let one of the guys in my crew crash at my pad for a few days while he found a new apartment. Prior to this, most of the times I hung out with this guy were when we were out dancing. **In his eyes I was always an energetic, crazy dancer and speaker.**

However, when he saw me in my chill mode at the pad he freaked out. One day he asked me **"Are you okay, man?"** I was fine I told him. He wasn't used to seeing the other side of me that listens to classical music on the radio while reading a book or drinking some wine. He thought maybe I was depressed or something! Ha!

We all have different shades of who we are. We are not perfect, although some people think they are! In order to truly know who you are you must be willing to accept who you are, every bit, not just the good things. Maybe you are like me and procrastinate too much. Perhaps you are forgetful or say things that you wish you could instantly take back. On the other end maybe you try too hard to be mean or detached, but in reality you are a genuinely nice person. **Don't be afraid to be who you are.**

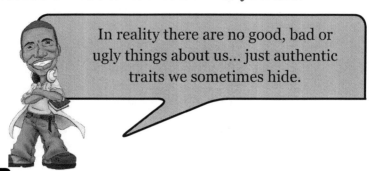

In reality there are no good, bad or ugly things about us... just authentic traits we sometimes hide.

Break Free

Now yes, there are some qualities we can improve on such as back-stabbing, lying, putting others down. Other people may even misread you and not know the real you because of some of the walls or defenses you put up.

Here is an exercise I have done that really helps you see yourself in a different light:

Think of your closest two or three friends or family members.

These should be people who you really trust, who know you with your strengths and faults, those who love you unconditionally.

Write their names down here and put one reason for why you value their opinion:

1. _

2. _

3. _

Break Free

Here is the fun part:

Write an email, send a text or write a letter with this question...

"What are 3 things about me or my actions that I may not be aware of that I could improve or work on?"

Let them know to be as honest as possible. Promise you won't key their car, un-friend them on Facebook or unfollow on Instagram or Twitter afterwards.

Now, you don't have to take everything they say to heart. However, you should look for patterns. **Are there things that more than one person is saying? Do some of these ring true for you as you think about it? Be honest!**

I did this exercise a few-years-ago and most of my closest friends were right on the money! The three consistent things they told me were:

- I flake too much (e.g. Say I'll do one thing, then cancel when something else comes up.)

- I say things that come across as hurtful or mean even if I am joking.

- I keep up a "safety wall" by not letting people get too close to me (e.g. sharing emotions.)

Remember, this is just an exercise to help you become more aware of some of the things that maybe you don't see. Our identity shouldn't be based on what others say, but there can be some truth if there is a consistency to all their replies.

Break Free

Accepting yourself can help you accept others

Accepting the true essence of who you are begins with knowing you are not perfect ;)

And that should be a relief!

Being at your best means knowing your strengths and where you can work on improving

So...

What are 2-3 things others say you need to be aware of about yourself?

One of the best ways to grow as a person is through **self-awareness** – which is the ability to look inward, to know how you are doing, your strengths, your challenges, your thoughts and your behaviors. This can offer direction forward.

Break Free

SEEING BETTER:

- *Your Quality World:* **Answer this through pictures:** *If my life was exactly as I would like it to be, these experiences, material things or activities would be part of it...*

1. _

2. _

3. _

- *Edit pictures & make a collage with www.picmonkey.com*

- *If you capture video, create a movie with www.magisto.com or the Magisto app (download on your phone) – use songs inspired from today! (You can use any photo or video editing software for this activity.)*

Break Free

Who You're Not

> *"I AM WHO I AM AND SAY WHAT I THINK. I'M NOT PUTTING A FACE ON FOR THE RECORD."*
>
> **-Eminem**

During middle school and high school I was 100% pure nerd. Now, this was when it wasn't trendy to be a nerd-this was the dark ages! Being a nerd meant bullies, taunting and random attacks by zombies (you know, being a nerd with a big brain and such made me extra tasty).

I didn't even have to try being a nerd, my nerdiness came authentically. In middle school I had crazy fluffy hair and sported my clarinet case with pride. In high school I carried my Bible around, was too shy to talk to the ladies and loved listening to classical music, big band music and reading tons of comic books.

My two best friends at the time had undergone a change for the worst. My close friends (whom I used to float down flooded creeks with, spend hours at the arcade with and re-enact Beavis and Butthead moments with) had joined a gang called the Outlaws. No longer were they the goofy friends I used to roll with. They were now faded shadows of the true persons they used to be. They wore a symbolic mask of being tough and untouchable.

Break Free

Gone were the days of eating cereal with orange juice instead of milk, placing road kill on my neighbor's doorsteps and daring each other to walk down the street in our tighty whities. They changed the fullness of who they were for the superficial acceptance of their gang.

When you start changing who you are for the acceptance of others then you are settling for a second rate version of yourself.

You are who you are and that is good enough (sounds like a Sesame Street quote, huh?) Embrace who you are and deny who you aren't. You are not a mistake, screw up or nobody. You are not the gum on the bottom of a worn out shoe, you are not just a dart board for others to throw painful insults at.

Being true to who you are may be challenging, but not as challenging as spending a lifetime trying to be someone you are not.

Break Free

As the American Poet E.E. Cummings said:

❝*It takes courage to grow up and
become who you really are.***❞**

**What are 3 things you can do to quit being
someone you're not?**

How can you begin revealing your true self?

*For example, I will not live in fear, I will stand up for
myself and others.*

I will:

I will:

I will:

SEEING BETTER:

- Take pictures of something that you think reflects some part of who you are **today, at this point of time in your life.**

- Take a picture of **things that you value;** what you think are **important** in your life or for the world.

- Take pictures of **something or some activity** that shows how you want to people to see you. ("When they think of me and my name, the first thing that will come to mind should be _____ .)"

Break Free

Break Free

I Know You and
You Know Me

> "IN SCHOOL I WAS SO COOL
> I KNEW THAT I COULDN'T CREASE EM
> MY FRIENDS COULDN'T AFFORD 'EM
> FOUR STRIPES ON THEIR ADIDAS
> ON THE COURT I WASN'T THE BEST
> BUT MY KICKS WERE LIKE THE PROS
> YO, I STICK OUT MY TONGUE SO EVERYONE
> COULD SEE THAT LOGO"

-Macklemore & Ryan Lewis "Wings"

I spend much of my time talking to young people and professionals about strategies that have been shown as effective for helping people lead the happiest lives possible. I like to think that I have always had the best judgment, been fair to everyone I came into contact with, and most of all had an identity that was not dependent on being better than others. "Ha wishful thinking!"

Sneakers... I know in some places they are called "tennis shoes," but I am from New York and we call them "sneakers." Anyway, sneakers have been a symbol of status for youth for a long time. They took on even greater status in the Michael Jordan era of the mid to late 1980s. He was an actual basketball player then. Yes, those "Jordans" that are so popular now and that come in a million different styles were only 1 single type of sneaker made by Nike back in those days. Today they are a brand of their own.

But back to the story. Even before Jordan's came on the scene, for kids, there was always a difference between name brand sneakers and what we called "Skips."

It was always better to know you had name brand sneakers whether it was Nike, Converse, Adidas, or even Pony. Pony's attempt to recreate their own version of Jordan's – the "City Wings" sneaker enjoyed some success, especially after Spud Webb –all five foot seven of him – shocked the world and won the 1986 NBA Slam Dunk contest while sporting a pair.

There was a certain joy at "rocking" a popular pair of sneakers. Run DMC even made a song about their favorite sneakers, "My Adidas!" You were somebody. You were not poor. You were cool. And you looked good! And there was also another level of joy at laughing at someone who had "Skips." You were somehow better than them.

I had a group of eight friends that I considered my best

Break Free

buddies as a kid. Anytime I was outside I was with one or more of the eight. We enjoyed hanging out playing all sorts of sports –like basketball, stickball, football, baseball- riding bikes, riding skateboards, playing hide and seek, tag, b-boying/breakdancing and a million other things that kids do for fun. We also liked to joke – and I mean joke all the time. We would tease each other in fun, but at times this "fun" would be at the expense of each other.

On one occasion, a little before the Jordan era, one of our friends had these strange new sneakers nobody had ever heard of and we gave him the business. We pointed, laughed, ridiculed, and generally made his day awful. He insisted that these were not "Skips" at all – but we knew better.

We were creative with the insults. We compared his sneakers to our own and joked about how much he wished he had some "real" sneakers. I felt good because nobody would ever laugh at my sneakers like this. I knew when people looked down at my feet, they would see I had cool sneakers. I felt cool... I felt faster... I felt more secure in my steps... and most importantly I felt "better" than those that had "Skips" – like our friend.

Several months later, I happened to notice the same sneaker as our friend's "Skips" while window shopping in Foot Locker. But, how could this be?! Nobody in our entire neighborhood had ever sported this sneaker. I never heard of this brand before. This was completely foreign to me. Up on the shelf next to the Nikes, Converses, Adidas and Pony's was that funny sneaker with the big "N" on it... the "Skips" my friend was wearing. I took the sneaker off the shelf to look more closely. The brand was called "New Balance."

I was living according to assumptions about what was good and bad. And this is even after always hearing what happens when you ASSUME! I also did not allow for the possibility of alternative truths outside of my current awareness (my friend had indeed told me "these are not Skips"). However, more importantly, what if they were? So what? I was creating a falsely inflated view of myself at the expense of others. I connected my ideas about who I am with the need to be better than others. I bought into status symbols as a reflection of me as a person. I was only beginning to scratch the surface of the true me.

The 3U Challenge: *"Unkind, Untrue, Unnecessary"*

As much as we seek to live joyful lives with a positive self-image - so do others.

Sometimes it is a challenge to recognize how "we" might influence the self-image of others.

Between now and next week, see how long you can go without saying something "unkind, untrue or unnecessary" to another person.

Break Free

It's Not You, It's Me...
I Think.

> *"I DON'T KNOW THE KEY TO SUCCESS, BUT THE KEY TO FAILURE IS TRYING TO PLEASE EVERYONE ."*
>
> **-Bill Cosby**

As the sizzling sounds of the Salsa band played in the background my gaze met hers. Nice. We exchanged contact information and my heart danced a few days later when I contacted her. Over the next few weeks we hit it off as we went out dancing and spent lots of time together...woooooo! Except for your parents, you know yourself better than anyone else. Duh. We sometimes tell ourselves that we need to be with someone to be happy. Not so, my little amigos. The best way to be happy is to be true to who you are. Don't mistake love for a feeling and don't forget to love yourself first.

About a month into our "relationship" I began to see things in her and me that were not healthy. I knew I didn't want to be with her, but I didn't want to be the jerk who broke things off. The phrase "It's not you, it's me" does hold truth to it, but in order to be authentically true to yourself there will be times where, yeah, you will have to say "It's not me, it's you."

Most of us, especially those of us who like everyone to like us, may suffer from a certain level of co-dependency. Pretty much this means you put the goodwill of others above your own goodwill. You seek their approval, you try to "save" them from their problems and feel worthless when you are not depended on.

Yes, we should care for others. However, when you are trying to make their lives better while yours becomes more miserable this is a sign of an unhealthy relationship. If you constantly do things so you can get the approval of others or "feel good" about yourself then perhaps this is a good time for a check up. Knowing who you are means embracing those things that are good and letting go of those things that aren't so good;

When we think of the question "Who Am I?" we can cause a lot of interference when we are constantly changing who we are for the person(s) we are with. We may do things out of a need for approval or because we think our opinion doesn't matter. You are who you are. Yes, improve yourself, but don't change the true version of yourself for the false approval of others.

As well, don't stay in a relationship (whether with friends significant other) just for the sake of being nice,

Break Free

thinking you can't do better or because you are trying to "save" the person. You are worth the best in life because you are the best. Holla.

Are you codependent? Take the test!

http://www.okcupid.com/tests/the-codependency-test

http://www.livestrong.com/article/14241-common-characteristics-of-codependence/

Break Free

Mistaken Identity?

> *"HAVE NO FEAR OF PERFECTION—YOU'LL NEVER REACH IT."*
>
> **-Salvador Dali**

When we hold onto past mistakes we are limiting our ability to reach for future possibilities. You are not a mistake. You will make mistakes, you will fail, you will have setbacks. Heck, you might even embarrass yourself epically in the process. The thing to remember is that mistakes can refine you, but don't let them define you. Learn from your actions and move on.

Before I ever got into B-Boying (e.g. break dancing) and the whole Hip Hop culture I was a grade A 100% band nerd. My senior year of high school I was representing my school and band mates in the U.I.L. competition. As part of this competition we were given different musical selections to play, each a different level of difficulty.

I had practiced my little heart out and kept a positive attitude (perhaps you've heard the same lie I did of "Practice makes perfect!" Ha!) The day of the competition went by in a flurry of nervousness and excitement. When it was my turn to play the most challenging piece of music

Break Free

I crumbled under the pressure. It also didn't help that the judges were about 5 feet in front of me and behind me was a room full of my fellow competitors. Suck!

To say I screwed up would be an understatement. I got the first few notes out on my clarinet and then everything fell apart. I made one mistake, went back, tried again, made the same mistake and then added a mistake. Ugh! It was like a snowball of fails growing with every new attempt. I finally stopped. Silence filled the room.

Now, this may not be the best piece of advice to follow, but I'll share it anyways. In my mind life is an adventure, the outcome is a result of what we put into it. During my moment of silence in that room I made the decision to walk away with an adventure. Whether I won or failed was no longer my main concern. *I decided to have a little fun.*

Ignoring the music that was in front of me I began to play some freestyle Jazz on my long, sleek clarinet. Soulful melodies replaced the technical and rigid sheet music that was in front of. As one of the judges screamed at me "No! No! No!" I knew I had done something, well, *different.* I finished my sidetracked show of band nerd rebellion and sat down. The room was all a buzz with whispers and grins. That was cool. *I turned my stupid mistake into a significant memory.*

When you make mistakes take them as learning experiences from a teacher you don't really like. Yeah, you may be embarrassed, heart broken or ridiculed, but what have learned from this experience? To hold onto past mistakes is to hold onto a fake image of who we are.

When we focus constantly on our mistakes we are letting a momentary failure keep us from a lifelong reality of success! Just because you fail a test, have a bad break up or fail to make the team does not mean you are any less of a person. I wish there was a "delete" button or something that we could use to forget our mistakes, but sadly there is not one...yet! (Still waiting for Google or Apple to make some type of brain implant!) What we focus on we will move towards.

If you are constantly focusing on your screw ups and mistakes then that will be your reality. If you can force yourself to move past those thoughts, you can be that awesome person that you know you really are! The only people who don't make mistakes are those people who never try.

Life is so exciting, rich and meaningful when you can take the chances to try something great. Making mistakes will keep you humble, but it should also keep you hungry to keep trying. You are not your mistakes.

Epic B-Boy Fails:

http://www.youtube.com/watch?v=uh9LGytJOHk

http://www.youtube.com/watch?v=-rC2qcx4iTY

http://www.youtube.com/watch?v=Ud09fainFXk

http://www.youtube.com/watch?v=wpqzukQJ1bU

Break Free

SEEING BETTER:

- Take pictures of parts of your life that make you the most proud

- Take pictures of areas of your life that you would like to have more influence over what happens

- *Edit pictures & make a collage with **www.pic monkey.com***

- *If you capture video, **create a movie with www .magisto.com** or the Magisto app (download on your phone) – use songs inspired from today! (You can use any photo or video editing software for this activity.)*

Break Free

Break Free

I Am Awesome

> *"I'D RATHER BE HATED FOR WHO I AM THAN LOVED FOR WHO I AM NOT."*
>
> -*Kurt Cobain | Nirvana*

Congratulations, you have made it to the last chapter! The good news is you can recycle this book, give it to someone for their birthday (don't expect that friendship to last long) or try selling it online. Now the bad news is I really don't know how to end this book. My brain shut down on this book project about 5 months ago. No, really. I was so stressed out about this book that I had to reach out to a best selling author by the name of Wes Lyons just to vent and whine!

After speaking with him I had a breakthrough! I decided to buckle down and get this book finished!! On a cold Friday afternoon I made a decision to tackle the final chapter of this book with everything left in my squishy brain. I was motivated! I was inspired! I was...so easily distracted. I ended up hanging out in another city with a fellow speaker, went dancing til 1 am, spent the next day eating pan dulce with friends, chilling at the lake, went crazy on some swings, beat the mess out of my friends with a huge palm branch, played catch in another park, danced

Break Free

the evening away with a live drum circle, played hackey sack with strangers, ate cake with my folks and watched the winter Olympics. Whew! So much for working on this book. Ha!

As this chapter is supposed to be all inspiring and contain the secret to life and stuff I guess I should take a stab at sending you on your merry way with some useful insight. So, here is your epic farewell speech--Dear Earthling, this is not the last chapter! There! Done! This book is over!! Yessss!! I can now spend countless hours watching old 1980's movies.

Yep, that's it. This is not the last chapter. This book has no last chapter for the simple reason that your life really doesn't have a last chapter. Who you become in this life is totally up to you. How you live your life will be totally up to you. I hope that at the end of each day you can be proud of the person you are and not be ashamed to show that person off to the world.

You will continually change over the next few seconds, minutes, hours, days and so on. Change for the better. Take the necessary steps you need to become the kind of person you want to be. I hope you can make sense out of all of this. Not just this book, but life. Don't let the circumstances or crap in this world affect who you are. It will be hard, it will be fun...stay true to who you are no matter what comes your way.

Smile when it's time to smile, but don't be afraid to cry when it is time to cry. I encourage you to write "I Am

Break Free

AwesoME" somewhere you can see it everyday. Write it on a mirror, on a binder, use it as a screen saver, whatever. **Don't change who you are for the acceptance of others.** True richness in life comes when you can be true to who you are and still have people who love you (even if you piss them off from time to time.)

There is no greater way to go through life than to do what you love, help others feel accepted and to be able to look in the mirror and truly say, "I am awesoME." Be true. Be you. Peace out!

It's not over yet, though! Hit us up! Let us know your thoughts on the book, ask any question you like, share your secret recipes, share a cool story, whatever! Let's stay in touch, for reals!

@raptjr
raphael@flowstory.org

@patrickpacman
patrick@patrickperez.org

Break Free

Excerpt from Bully Breakthrough:

It was yet another fun-filled day in math (yeah, I'm being sarcastic) and David was getting his daily dose of flicking my ear again and again. This time he was talking trash the whole time just for added value. I asked him to stop, I tried ignoring him and nothing worked. Finally, much like Casey "Hulk" Heynes, I snapped. David hit my ear one too many times and I made sure this would be his last time!

Since he was sitting behind me I spun my upper body around as fast as I could with my arm extended. My closed fist hit his arm with such force that I am sure his arm went numb. My adrenaline was pumping, my fist still clenched. The flicking stopped.

For some odd reason it never dawned on me to get the teacher involved. I guess there is a certain pride or fear of retaliation that keeps us silent.

My biggest mistake was thinking that nobody cared if I got picked on. And for this reason I often kept quiet.

Preview more for free or download today Amazon.com!

Doc's Back 2 School Toolkit
(can download at flowstory.org)

The attached toolkit is to inspire reflection and action by new and returning students alike... This is also for people in a position to be a positive support to new and returning students. The goal is to encourage greater attention to positive growth as a person and as a student.

It is meant to allow us to reflect upon how we see ourselves as students, and how we envision our role in the fabric of our school and our social circles.

Inside you will find:

1. Meaningful quotes from some of Hip-Hop's most respected artists, meant to touch on important themes of growth in general, but with a specific link to being a student.

2. Thoughtful questions and notes to guide your reflection on areas of life as a student

3. Vibrant and colorful images that speak to these themes

4. Suggested resources to help take action in areas you feel are important

5. 20 additional in-depth reflection and discussion questions that can be used with one person or in group of students; guaranteed to move you toward being a #BetterStudent

6. A list of more than 20 powerful songs to help you explore these areas in more detail.

51878472R00037

Made in the USA
San Bernardino, CA
04 August 2017